TO LOVE DELILAH

Claiming the Women
of the Bible

TO LOVE DELILAH

Claiming the Women
of the Bible

by

Mary Cartledge-Hayes

San Diego, California

LuraMedia™

© Copyright 1990 LuraMedia
San Diego, California
International Copyright Secured
Publisher's Catalog Number LM-618
Printed and Bound in the United States of America

Illustrations by Adriana Diaz
Book design by Maryam Gossling

LuraMedia, Inc.
7060 Miramar Road, Suite 104
San Diego, CA 92121

Library of Congress Cataloging-in-Publication Data

Cartledge-Hayes, Mary.
    To love Delilah : claiming the women of the Bible / by Mary Cartledge-
       Hayes.
      p. cm.
    Bibliography: p.
    ISBN 0-931055-68-7
    1. Women in the Bible.   2. Women--Religious life.   I. Title.
    BS575.C34   1990
    2220.9'2'082--dc20   90-35856
                                                      CIP

All Scripture quotations unless otherwise indicated are from the Revised
Standard Version of the Holy Bible, copyright 1946, 1952, and © 1971, 1973 by the
Division of Christian Education, National Council of the Churches of Christ in
the U.S.A. and used by permission.

The following pieces originally appeared in a slightly different form in
Daughters of Sarah: "The Pillar" (January/February 1988) and "What Child IS
This?" (November/December 1984). "Delilah's Side" appeared in slightly differ-
ent form in *The Witness* (July/August 1987).

For my parents,

Douglas and Joanna Belle Cartledge,

and in memory of

Helen Loomis Storr and Lucille Westfall

Acknowledgments

I owe moments of confirmation and revelation to the writings of Denise Lardner Carmody, Carol P. Christ, Mary J. Evans, Elisabeth Schüssler Fiorenza, Nancy Hardesty, Elisabeth Moltmann-Wendel, Rosemary Radford Ruether, and Letha Scanzoni. I owe moments of affirmation and confirmation to the articulate faith, steadfast encouragement, and occasional proddings of Meg Barnhouse, Monnie Cannon, Nancy Hardesty, Anne Herbert, Nicole Jensen-Oost, Nancy Moore, Mary Flowers McCarter, and Susan Phifer Johnson. I name them in recognition of those women who are nameless due to the darkness of deliberate exclusion.

My special thanks to Tara Flowers, Jennifer Flowers, Debbie Hayes, Steve Hayes, Fred Hayes, Jr. — and to my husband, Frederick B. Hayes.

I also thank those I can't name whose inclusive love and faith sustained me in the year this book came into being.

Contents

Introduction

Aren't the things we notice as children peculiar? Take the women of the Bible. The four who have stuck with me are Eve, Lot's wife, Delilah, and Mary the mother of Jesus.

To me as a child, Mary didn't count; for all intents and purposes she fell off the face of the earth once she climbed down from that donkey in Bethlehem and had that baby. Thus my earliest and strongest awareness of the rest of the Bible women was of failures: the evil, the irrational, the unfaithful.

I never thought of this as a problem. I knew only that I had a fierce resistance to reading the Bible, a resistance lodged in an unwillingness to involve myself intimately with a document that had so little good to say about women.

Over time I learned there were political reasons for my negative impression of biblical women. God-loving people in the early (and later) centuries of the church found it expedient or vital to reaffirm the structures of patriarchy in spite of Jesus' explicit affirmation of women.

Over time I came to understand that the women of the Bible are largely single-issue characters. While many men get chapters, even books devoted to their stories, women's stories elicit a sentence or two. They are adjunct to the primary (male, important) stories. Women appear long enough for someone to make a point and then disappear in a puff of smoke — literally in the case of Samson's wife. We don't know what size sandals they wore, how they felt about their hair, or what their favorite colors were. Our connection to them is tenuous, making them easy to stereotype, hardly worth the struggle to understand.

13

Over time I came to see that what I remembered from childhood came under the heading "popular wisdom." Popular wisdom is seldom wise and is more often mythological than biblical. The stories I knew were interpretations woven by storytellers who left out some important details and embroidered others. When distortion was necessary to make a square peg fit a round hole, storytellers whittled.

One particularly depressing afternoon, I was horrified to find that, for all my respect for and appreciation of the godliness of women, I had internalized the myths. Wedged in a dank corner of my mind was the notion that women are fundamentally flawed.

Look at us: we eat apples, we look back, we seduce God's chosen. We are The Other our forefathers warned us about.

As Zora Neale Hurston says in *Their Eyes Were Watching God*, "It was like seeing your sister turn into a 'gator. A familiar strangeness. You keep seeing your sister in the 'gator, and the 'gator in your sister, and you'd rather not."[1]

The familiar strangeness was uncomfortable enough to make me explore the dualism in Christianity that places God on one side and the Bible on the other. God teaches me to love myself; the Bible, to despise women. Should I throw God out the window like the smelly baby in Punch and Judy? Should I burn my Bible? Must I have a sex-change operation to be a real Christian?

I am a woman, and my faith creates a conflict. Because of this I find wisdom and solace in the writings of women who are leaving Christianity behind as they search for a more affirmative faith. Like Zsuzsanna E. Budapest, I think we must create and use self-blessings "to change the influences working in our deep minds,"[2] the notion that we are lesser creations. Like Nelle Morton, I'm "saying no to those images, symbols, structures, and practices that cripple us and keep us from claiming our rightful personhood."[3]

Yet I don't plan to leave the Christian fold. I believe that's where the answers to my spiritual questions lie. Partly I'm stubborn. I don't intend to be shoved out of my faith by those who would be content with my alms and my body while ignoring my mind and my voice. More than that, however, I stay because of the truth I find, and the joy. That leaves me with two choices: to deny and ignore the dualism, or to address it and learn what I can.

I choose the latter. I'm naming the stereotypes and confronting the myths. What am I finding? Not wicked women but human beings, thinking, breathing, living women in tough situations who made the best choices they could at the time.

Interviewed on the publication of *The Woman's Bible*, Susan B. Anthony said, "Of course people say these women [its authors] are impious and presumptuous for daring to interpret the Scriptures as they understand them, but I think women have just as good a right to interpret and twist the Bible to their own advantage as men always have twisted and turned it to theirs."[4]

This is not to say I've twisted anything. Men and women live different lives, and in this book I'm standing at the intersection of the Bible and popular culture, looking to see how it looks to a woman.

The result is not a traditional Bible study. I mingle biblical accounts with stuff I made up. I take things out of context and unabashedly address the stories in the light of my own white middle-class twentieth-century American experience. I offer integrative activities intended to help apply insights gained to daily life.

I still remember the pain I heard in the voice of a Canadian woman speaking at Forum '85, a conference held in Nairobi, Kenya, to mark the end of the United Nations' Decade for Women. She said, "I alternate between despair and the feeling we're taking a few small steps." I hope this book is a small step.

Eve

And the moral of the story is: women are the root of all evil.

Popular Wisdom

God created Adam. Then God created Eve to serve Adam. God plunked them down in the Garden of Eden where nobody ever argued, itched, complained, or left dirty clothes on the floor.

"Leave my apples alone," God said.

"Okay," said the first couple.

Time ambled past, with nobody able to remember what day it was because nothing occurred to separate one moment from the next.

One day Adam and Eve went for a walk. They planned to turn left at the apple tree, but, as sometimes happens, they stopped to talk to an acquaintance and got sidetracked.

"Want an apple?" asked the snake.

"Oh, gee, I don't know," said Eve. "I really shouldn't. What do you think, Adam?"

Adam didn't say a word.

"Oh, come on," said the snake. "It'll be a whole new taste sensation. Give it a shot."

"Shall I, Adam?"

Adam didn't say a word.

"What can it hurt?" asked the snake.

Eve took the apple.

Adam didn't say a word.

Eve bit into the apple.

Adam didn't say a word.

"Yummy," said Eve. "Adam, would you like a bite?"

"Yes, thanks," said Adam.

And he too ate from the apple.

God was furious. He condemned the snake to belly crawling and tossed the first family out of the garden. God was especially angry with Eve, advising her that in punishment women would suffer pain in childbirth and earn only 60 cents on the dollar for the next multithousand years. This was fair because it was all Eve's fault.

And the moral of the story is: women are the root of all evil.

From the Garden

What was it like
when I was young?
First off, nothing slithered.
Your dad and I walked ten miles
to the stream and back
each day without complaining.
Everything that could sing did.

How has it changed?
Roars took the place of purrs,
and fear that never was is now.
Lambs and lions flee
when they hear me laugh.
Everything still knows my name,
but none will call.

Was it worth it?
No. It never is.

How has it changed?
When I could no longer talk to birds,
I had time to spend on other things.
See this leaf? Once it was wild.
Now it's tame, even as it cages my body.
See this rock? Whether cold or warm
it's always stiff. That's a thing worth knowing.
Look in the pond. See the shadows?
I didn't when I was young.

Was it worth it?
Yes, because this is life,
and there are wonders enough
to ease the pain.

What's the biggest difference?
You'll learn that for yourselves,
but, if you insist, I'll tell you this:
now I have to listen
to hear the songs.

* * * * *

If women accept popular wisdom regarding Eve and the business in the garden, we might as well throw our hands in the air and give up on spirituality altogether. Classic interpretations of the creation story could not be more clear: woman is the cause of sin and degradation. Without Eve, Adam would still be puttering around in the garden, naked and pure. In sinning, Eve set the precedent for all women. We can never atone for her actions, but, if we get lucky, God may overlook our gender.

This is not my interpretation when I'm alert. It's what I'd mumble if you asked me very early in the morning, before I'm awake enough to be sensible, or when I'm over-tired and need a nap. It's the *National Enquirer* rendition of reality, a summary of innuendo, undercurrents, and whispers. It's what I've heard the Bible says.

Oddly enough, this vision of women and God was hawked for centuries. Since women have begun translating original texts and finding or creating publication outlets, however, alternate interpretations are appearing — interpretations often closer to Scripture, more logical, and more kind.

Analyses are readily available, but I'll summarize them anyhow. Repetition is necessary. Otherwise, just as in libel cases where the publisher retracts a page-one headline in page-ten small print, hurtful rumors may have eternal life.

First, the issue of domination. "Women are meant to clean toilets because they're secondary rib tissue, not primary male," goes the popular doctrine. "Popular" does not equal "valid," however. Genesis 1 states that man and woman were created at the same time. No domination can be explicated from that version. Genesis 2 supposedly claims Adam as the primary creation, the epitome of God's handiwork. Yet God created Adam; God then created fish, fowl, cattle, and cockroaches; God then created Eve. Logically, therefore, Eve should be revered as the culmination of creation.

Not possible, say male scholars. She came from Adam's rib.

Big deal. Adam came from dirt. Furthermore, God didn't say, "Hey, Adam, why don't you make yourself a woman?" God sent Adam to Sleepytown, and God created.

Isn't it odd that nobody uses this information to claim Eve as the superior being?

Impossible, some say, because of the apple business. Eve's at fault there.

Yes. But Adam ate of the apple, too. He, like the other adult around at the time, was responsible for his action. God didn't name one person and one reptile as culprits and excuse the third participant. God punished the snake for its deception, and God expelled the pair from the garden to save them from immortality.

The problem with the creation story, then, is not the story. The problem is the myth that has grown up around it and the effects of that myth on succeeding generations.

My tenth-grade daughter has a list her history teacher Mark Taylor and his colleagues compiled. The topic under discussion was woman's rights. This is an abridged version of their "Arguments Used Against Women in History."

1. Women have smaller brains and are therefore less intelligent than men.

2. Women shouldn't attend college because they're not strong enough physically.

3. Women are the weaker sex, and therefore men need to protect them.

4. Women can't handle responsibility because they can't make rational decisions.

5. Women are not good at handling money; therefore, men should control financial matters.

6. Men can make the best decisions concerning the welfare of women.

This was for a history class. Why not current events? Are all these notions dead and gone? I think not. I think they're underground but still viable. Also I think two additional arguments have a place on the list:

7. Women can't be president because when they have their periods they get peevish and might blow up the world.

8. Women can't preach because they sinned first.

Such arguments thrive in the soil of a creation myth that says Eve — and all women since — are the root of all evil.

What happens to self-esteem when women internalize such a revolting myth? It predisposes us to live our lives in shadows.

I've committed some walloping mistakes. I can recall each in withering detail because for years I carried them with me. Whether I was peeling onions, writing a poem, or making a bank deposit, they sang to me. They sounded like this:

I'm not doing this right.

I don't know how to do this.

Someone else could do this better.

I'm not making sense.

I'm going to fail.

I'm a miserable human being.

The fact that such thinking is contrary to my faith didn't interrupt my self-abasement. I couldn't see the conflict between belief in a loving God and my assumption that I was a failure.

I'm not unusual in this regard. In her book *Love and Be Loved*,[1] Marie Chapian describes the time she asked a congregation to stop saying ugly things about themselves for ten days. Everyone in the group agreed to try. Everyone failed. This suggests that self-critical comments are a natural (although not innate) mode of reflection. Breaking that cycle seems especially difficult for women — because we are tacitly encouraged to think poorly of ourselves, because society is notorious for denigrating us, and because our lives, being more diverse, offer more opportunities for self-blame if we're so inclined.

Self-criticism works like a spot of water in the basement that becomes a trickle that becomes a river that becomes a flood that becomes a major repair bill. Stopping, for me, took self-awareness first and self-discipline second. It also took faith.

Faith tells us that God breathes goodness into each person. To believe in God and at the same time to consider women lesser creations is an abomination.

Despising Eve trivializes God. Can I expect wisdom from a God who created me so I could ruin the world? Can I expect help from a God who created me to help someone who scorns me? Can I expect comfort from a God who defines me by one mistake? Can I love a God who created me evil? Can I honestly believe in that God?

No, honestly, I can't. The God I know is not petty, mean, or indifferent. The God I know convinces me that I make mistakes, but I am not my mistakes. This God lets me know that I'm not perfect, and that it's okay. I'm human.

Keeping my focus on this God makes room for a new vision of Eve, perhaps like the persona in the poem at the beginning of this chapter. That Eve is ambivalent about where life has taken her. She knows the costs of her mistakes. Yet she has come to accept that God created her fallible and good. She accepts life, and she accepts herself.

* * *

God can be an antidote to self-negativity. Thus these activities are designed to help us live more intentionally, noticing and celebrating God's presence in our lives.

Decide to Read the Bible

It's time we talked less and read more. The problem, it seems to me, is not so much desire as getting started. Try this method.

1. *Consider the potential difficulties and pleasures.*

In a group or alone with a notebook, reflect on what reading the Bible means to you. Use these questions as starting points: What interferes with my doing so? Am I resistant, resentful, forgetful? Am I too busy? State your reasons. Then consider what you might gain from reading the Bible. Information? A sense of accomplishment? A better understanding of God? State your reasons.

2. *Plan your approach.*

Perhaps you've never read the Bible through completely. In that case, you may decide to read through the New Testament or the Prophets one book a week, or to complete your reading in a specific time period (one year, six months). Your goal may be to get in the habit of daily Bible reading. Decide what you want to accomplish.

3. *Plan your method.*

How can you best build Bible reading into your life? Reading at the same time every day helps. What's easiest for you? When are your distractions fewest? Choose.

4. *Intend to read the Bible.*

Make it a commitment. Say it, write it down, tell a friend, or think it — but in some way affirm to yourself that you will do it.

5. *Enjoy.*

Pick a focus that will make it a pleasure for you. Are you looking for the women hidden behind patriarchal attitudes? Are you looking for evidence of miracles? Are you looking for verses you might want to memorize? Be kind to yourself. Don't fret if you miss a day. It will still be there the next day.

Lot's Wife

And the moral of the story is: women are stupid.

Popular Wisdom

God was sick and tired of Sodom and Gomorrah. Sin surged like a flooding river, depositing wickedness on every doorstep.

"I'll destroy these places," God decided, "and all the inhabitants except Lot and his family."

Lot, an obedient man, didn't hesitate to follow God's command. He whisked his family off to the hills where they would be safe.

"Don't look back! Don't look back!" God urged. "Something terrible will happen."

Unfortunately, Lot's wife ignored him. She was too dumb to recognize the danger, or too sinful to want salvation, or too attached to her possessions.

So God turned her into a pillar of salt.

And the moral of the story is: women are stupid.

The Pillar

Even to the nameless dog I said farewell.
Madness took him long since,
but I remember his sharp bark,
how he warmed my feet on cool evenings.
I nursed my father in that city,
raised a cup to his lips the night he died.
We laid him near the fig tree,
its twisted trunk his monument.

Now ash marks his place, and Mother's too,
and all the others whose bread sometimes burnt,
whose clay pots shattered, who wept with me.
They were not good people, and yet . . .
Lot's back was not enough to see.
I turned. One sigh, one glance
for all we left behind.
My faith is strong —
yea, stronger even than salt.
I wait for God to forgive my love.

* * * * *

There's more to the tale of Lot and his wife than popular wisdom would have us believe. This is the full story of the destruction of Sodom, from Genesis 19:

God sent two angels to Sodom. The original plan had been to destroy the city entirely, but Abraham convinced God to spare any righteous people who lived there, if there were any, which God doubted.

Lot happened to be sitting by the town gate when the angels approached.

"Come on over to my house, strangers," said Lot. "You can wash your feet and get a good night's sleep."

After some argument, the angels agreed.

The townspeople were suspicious of this arrangement (their paranoia, in fact, proved justified). They demanded that Lot send his guests outside.

"Oh, please," begged Lot, "take my virgin daughters and rape them instead. Just don't bother my guests."

The angry townspeople began to pummel Lot. The angels came to his rescue, dragged him to safety, and blinded the people outside.

The angels knew they'd found their righteous man. "Flee!

31

Flee!" they said to Lot. "God sent us to destroy this miserable town. Get out while you still can!"

Lot was impressed enough by their urgency to go hunting for his sons-in-law (marriage laws were different then; these young men carried the title although the marriages had not yet been consummated). Lot wanted to offer his sons-in-law the chance to escape, but mostly he wanted their opinions on the angels.

"Get real," they said.

The next morning found the angels still pleading with Lot, and Lot still not moving.

Finally the angels were tired of arguing. They had a big day ahead and didn't want to get stuck working overtime, so they grabbed Lot, his wife, and the two unraped daughters by the arms and deposited them outside the city.

"Head for the hills," said the angels.

"Aw, gee," said Lot, "can't I just go to that little town over there instead?"

"All right, already. Just move it, will you?"

Off they went. God sent sulfur and fire raining down on Sodom like bombs over Dresden. Lot and his daughters escaped. His wife, however, looked back and was turned into a pillar of salt.

Lot and his daughters survived, and so did Lot's family tree. His daughters got him drunk and lay with him, resulting in the births of Moab and Ben-ammi, who became heads of the Moabites and Ammonites, respectively.

What an interesting story, and what interesting conclusions have been drawn from the single sentence about Lot's wife in the text. Edith Deen, in her landmark book *All of the Women of the Bible*, assumes that Lot's wife is "a worldly, selfish woman" who "love[d] the things of the world more than the things of the spirit" and whose daughters' "later relations with their father were a blot on their mother's character."[1]

Deen's conclusions reflect attitudes toward women that have changed over the past few decades. Mother-bashing (the tendency to blame the mother for her children's actions) hasn't been outlawed, but it is at least suspect. I can thus state what now seems obvious: Lot's daughters are responsible for their own actions.

If the message of the story is that God's punishment is swift and forceful, it seems to me the wrong victim died. Lot dragged his feet. He consulted with the sons-in-law. He loitered. He whined about his destination. If God meant to respond to disobedience, why not Lot's?

That brings us to the subject of Lot's wife's love of possessions. This is the part of the story that I think has a direct and immediate application to our lives.

The love of possessions is as American as jazz, baseball, and buttered grits. Conspicuous consumption keeps our labor force employed and our economy strong. The downside is that values get skewed, and we face insider trading on Wall Street, an ethics crisis in business, children killed on city streets in the low-overhead, high-profit drug wars, and offshore workers exploited to keep the price of our affluence down. In a society where the consumer is king, charge cards become chalices and possessions become sacraments. The story of Lot's wife, if we choose to view her as greedy and selfish, can well be considered, in light of our shopping habits, as a warning.

There's another side of her story, however, one that I can explain best by telling about my house fire.

Two days after Christmas, two of my children smelled smoke at 5:53 p.m. At 5:54 I called the fire department. At 5:55 we were hurrying down our driveway, all the children barefoot, all of us empty-handed except the nineteen-year-old who was carrying the dog.

At 8:30 we were allowed back into the house to lift purses and wallets from dressers and to board up the windows. We went to a friend's house to spend the night. She lent me a nightgown. The next morning I borrowed a pair of underpants from her.

We lived in a motel for three months while our house was being rebuilt. We occupied ourselves in the interim by throwing things away.

We threw away our seven hand-made Christmas stockings, our six graduation robes, my stashes of old letters, my three daughters' doll collections, and my address book. The wall calendars dating from 1979 went, too. On them I'd recorded swim meets and weddings, basketball games and births, church picnics, trips abroad, funerals, orthodontist appointments, and the day Bubba the hamster died. I hadn't saved them because I needed them but because I had recognized obscurely that our five children would not always be so young nor our lives so complex.

We threw away our Christmas ornaments, too, but not until after I'd spent hours at the kitchen sink scrubbing them with a toothbrush. As I scrubbed, I looked back to the first days of my marriage to Fred, when we were innocent of the pressures and joys involved in committing ourselves to living together in the company of a twenty-year-old, an eight-year-old, and three teenagers. I thought of the years before, and the time since, and how we'd all stretched and been stretched in the process.

I went through a time when possessions didn't interest me. I owned two sweaters, a pair of good black wool pants, a pair of jeans, and two pairs of shoes. They were enough.

Now I have a cautious appreciation for the possessions that reside with me, and a certain understanding of why Lot's wife looked back. I don't think she was motivated by greed or stupidity but by love: the love she felt for others, the love of a hometown that was a place of relationship, the love of the security in seeing the same faces at the well day after day, of sharing the births and deaths of children, of hearing the same chickens scratching in the dirt and the same dogs barking for a bite of food.

Whether we live in opposition to it or affirmation of it, home colors our choices and energizes our decisions. To leave without a moment's pause is to deny that what has gone before has opened us to the present.

Edith Deen says of Lot's wife that she "so loved the city on which God was raining fire from heaven that she willingly gave her life

34

for it."[2] Does this make her a heroine or a fool, a model of greed or of love?

I find her a woman of possibilities.

* * *

Live Deliberately Among Your Possessions

Choose one of these exercises:

1. *Keep track of the money you spend for one month.*

Use a small notebook or pocket diary with large spaces. At the end of the month, consider these questions: Is it easier to spend money than to keep track of it? Did your attitude toward money change? Are you dismayed or pleased to learn where your money went?

2. *Check out your surroundings.*

One method is to do the household inventory insurance companies are always recommending. Another is to spend the weekend cleaning out closets, kitchen drawers, attic, and basement. Reflect on which items you need, use, or love. What gives them their value? What about the items you don't use? Why do you keep them? What possessions are necessary for your happiness?

3. *Decide not to buy any clothes for one year.*

I've considered this for three months and decided not to do it, even after adding qualifications. (Do shoes count? No. Does underwear? No. What if I need something for a special occasion? That doesn't count, either.) The longer I contemplate, the more I learn about myself. Ask: what does this tell me about myself? About my image? About materialism? About priorities?

Delilah

And the moral of the story is: women are traitors.

Popular Wisdom

God sent Samson, the pure of heart, to deliver Israel from the Philistines. One day Samson wandered over to the next valley and there fell in love with a woman named Delilah.

Delilah pretended to love Samson, but she was deceiving him. The Philistines had offered her 1100 shekels for discovering the secret to Samson's strength. The wench agreed to betray her lover.

Samson tried to withstand Delilah's trickery. First he told her that if he were tied up with seven fresh bowstrings, he would be weakened. So she tied him up with seven fresh bowstrings and called in the Philistines.

"Ha!" said Samson. "Fooled you!" And he burst his bonds.

So Delilah asked again.

"If I'm tied up with new ropes, I'll be weakened," he said.

Delilah found new ropes, tied him up, and called the Philistines.

"Ha!" said Samson. "Gotcha again!" And he burst his bonds.

So Delilah asked again.

"Weave my hair into a web," said Samson, "and fasten it with a pin."

So Delilah did. Again she called the Philistines. Again Samson broke free.

Delilah was tired of this game, but so, apparently, was Samson. This time when asked he told the truth: "If you shave my head, I will lose my strength."

Delilah informed the Philistines, who paid her off. Delilah waited until Samson went to sleep and then called in a barber, who turned Samson into a skinhead. The Philistines burst in, captured their prey, poked out his eyes, and threw him in jail.

Things worked out for the best. The Philistines forgot that even the worst haircut eventually grows out. They brought their prize prisoner into their temple to show him off. Samson responded by knocking down two load-bearing pillars, killing 3,000 of them and one of himself.

And the moral of the story is: women are traitors.

Delilah's Side

They say don't sleep
with a man crazier
than yourself.
What if it's
too late?

He never mentioned God.
He spoke only of himself
and how the smoke seered his eyes
and the smell of vengeance
and three hundred flaming foxes.
The foxes burned the olives,
burned the vineyards,
burned the standing fields
and the wheat already stored.
That woman his wife —
the woman he claimed
but never knew — was blamed
for choices she never made.
Thirty dirty screaming men
sacrificed her, and so did Samson.

Even without
the promise of shekels
I would betray him.

* * * * *

Delilah symbolizes women's basic failing. She teaches that we cannot be trusted because we will use our feminine abilities — our sensuality, our sexuality, our fertility, our listening ears, whatever other wiles we possess — to deceive.

Delilah's sisters are legion: the women who betray politicians by whispering state secrets, or businessmen by selling corporate secrets; the girls who betray the boy next door by getting pregnant. Character, honor, and integrity (not to mention contraception) all seem to be lacking.

Men tend to remember Delilah's myth when the unexpected occurs. After confiding their secrets or their sperm, they're shocked to find a consequence, and they're certain they've been had. Women, they conclude, will take advantage . . . will smile while the barber snips. But what, after all, can one expect from the second sex?

Intellectually, we know this is absurd, but it's an absurdity we measure ourselves against. Part of breaking the cycle is remembering the events that preceded Samson's meeting Delilah.

Here they are, from Judges 14 and 15:

One day Samson wandered into a village named Timnah. There he saw a Philistine maiden (note: this is not Delilah; this is another woman). Samson liked the way she looked, so he went home and said to his mom and dad: "I want her. Get her for me."

41

His parents were not pleased. Their son was a gift from God, his incipient conception announced by an angel who insisted, "No razor shall come upon his head, for the boy shall be a Nazirite to God from birth; and he shall begin to deliver Israel from the hand of the Philistines" (Judg. 13:5). In exchange, God granted Samson immense strength. Samson's parents couldn't understand how their son's marriage to a Philistine would fix Israel's problems, but they hated to argue. They agreed to the marriage.

A wedding feast was held, at which Samson proposed a riddle for thirty Philistine men. If they guessed correctly, Samson would provide a prize for each of them; if not, they would each give Samson a robe.

The thirty men must have really wanted to win. They paid a visit to Samson's intended and made a modest proposal: she would tell them the answer to the riddle, or they would set fire to her father's house and to her.

The woman apparently considered her options: to be hated by thirty Philistines who knew her address or by one Samson. Maybe she concluded there was power in numbers. In any case, she got Samson to tell her the answer to the riddle.

Samson was furious when the Philistines answered his riddle. Yet he wanted to be fair. Under God's direction, he stomped into a neighboring town, killed thirty men, stole their possessions, and handed them over to the Philistines. Then he went home, deserting his wife. She, now worthless on the matrimonial market, was handed off to another man.

Some time later Samson got to thinking about his wife again and decided she really was the love of his life. He returned to Timnah to claim her and was enraged to learn that she hadn't been kept for him. So he caught three hundred foxes, tied them tail to tail, put torches between their tails, and let them loose to fire the land.

The blaze burned everything: the land, the stored grain, the orchards, the food, and the promise of food for years to come.

A contented Samson went on his way, eventually to meet Delilah.

Thirty discontented Philistines set fire to Samson's wife and to her father.

After thinking about this story, I was very angry. Samson, by any recognizable standard, is a jerk. Loved by God he undoubtedly was, but what of the woman of Timnah? She was one leg of a hate triangle — and the leg most easily broken.

Her life was ruined because one day some guy happened to walk by and notice her. Imagine her alarm when thirty men surrounded her, demanding she conspire with them. Imagine her fear when she was handed off to some other man, her horror when Samson returned to destroy her people's livelihood. And imagine her terror when the thirty Philistines came back to break their promise.

I imagined it all, and I came up furious and filled with rhetorical questions. Who hushed up this story? Who decided Samson was a hero? Who weighed Samson's cruelty and Delilah's sneakiness and proclaimed Delilah the villain? This was a plot, I decided, a deliberate, nasty plot to degrade women, with coconspirators numbering in the millions.

Instead of hating Delilah, I now hated Samson, the thirty Philistines, my Sunday school teachers from second grade on, and every minister who contributed to the deceit from the pulpit. It didn't help when I learned at long last that my evaluation of Samson was realistic, that "the story of Samson found in Judges was intended to portray him as a negative religious leader and as an example *not* to follow."[1] Who knows that? Who remembers? Samson isn't cited in comments about politicians who are "womanizers" (by the way, wouldn't the term "lecher" be more appropriate for those public servants?), nor is his cruelty acknowledged.

My sympathies lodged squarely with Delilah, creating a new dilemma. I no longer hated her, but what was there of value in her story? Samson's wicked behavior neither excuses nor justifies hers. Besides, I was conditioned to despise her. How could I break that old habit of judging?

I followed my thinking around corners and up trees and through the woods until it came out the other side. On that other side was a possibility. What if Delilah knew of Samson's exploits in Timnah?

43

If that were the case, Delilah's "sin" was that she reacted inappropriately for a woman. She didn't choose to be longsuffering, to support Samson through right and wrong, to regret that she had but one life to give for her man. She was a woman who had to provide for herself in a community that used and despised her, a woman who would too soon grow old, a woman of dependent means, a woman who may have been afraid for her life.

Samson's wife typifies the terrible powerlessness of women; Delilah typifies the fact that women may be powerless, but they don't always have to die as a result. Sometimes they get lucky: they escape with only the hatred of generations to come.

Considering Delilah's life from this perspective is a helpful tool. It scatters the dark clouds of myth by suggesting that the empress may have been wearing clothes after all, clothes of reason or fear or choice that gawking spectators, blinded by their own needs to judge, could not see.

It tells me that other women — the ones who sell secrets and the ones who get pregnant — are also clothed. The choices they make may be bad or mad or unseemly, but their choices are the result of human reckoning, which, for all our attempts to live honorably, is still often bad, mad, or unseemly.

We are human. We make mistakes.

Understanding this in the lives of the notorious and the newsmakers prods us to understand it in the lives of strangers, acquaintances, and friends. It can release us from our eternal need to judge the good, the bad, and the different. It allows us to accept human error. More to the point, it prods us to understand it in the context of our own lives.

To love Delilah? Maybe in the final analysis the only way we can do so is to confront the parts of ourselves that remind us of her myth: the too-pragmatic parts, the deceitful parts, the frightened parts.

To be free to love Delilah, maybe we must first be free to love ourselves.

* * *

Choose to Love Yourself

We are continually choosing how to regard ourselves. Do we notice the tasks completed or the tasks left undone? Do we dwell on the lumps in today's potatoes or congratulate ourselves on the crispness of the fried chicken? What messages fill our minds?

We can choose not to live with self-criticism. Try these steps:

1. *Record your thinking.*

Over the period of three days, write down each negative thought you have about yourself. Evaluate your patterns. Are you harsher when you're tired or rushed? Do certain situations trigger negativity?

2. *Decide to be kind.*

Make a commitment that, for the period of one week, when you begin to think meanly of yourself, you will stop.

3. *Plan a replacement.*

The best way to rid ourselves of a habit is to find a replacement. Decide what you will replace your negative thoughts with. Choose something simple: a phrase such as "all is well" or "grace equal to every need."

4. *Record the changes.*

Is it difficult to replace the negative thoughts? Why? What do they accomplish, if anything? What happens when you refuse them? Do you think God prefers your criticism or your appreciation of yourself?

5. *Be kind.*

Don't be frustrated if you're not perfect at this on the first day. It takes time to break the cycle of negativity. The point of the exercise is to recognize that you are part of God's good creation.

Jezebel

And the moral of the story is: women are worthless.

Popular Wisdom

Jezebel wore too much eye makeup, and she slept around.

And the moral of the story is: women are worthless.

After the Fall

Will somebody get
these damned dogs
away from me, please?
The noise is awful —
all the snarling,
tearing and growling.
Oh, never mind.
I don't feel anything.
I can be grateful for that.
It's as Elijah said:
God can set you free
or kill you, depending.
Seems odd to me that death
can prove God's love,
but maybe I heard wrong.
When you're in the middle
it's hard to tell the difference
between love and hate.
Will someone get
these damned dogs
away from me?
Oh, never mind.

* * * * *

I conducted a mini-poll on Jezebel the other day.

"What do you know about her?" I asked a friend who grew up in the Baptist tradition and is currently active in her church.

"Her name," was the reply.

"Anything else?"

"Just that she was a terrible person."

That sums up attitudes toward Jezebel very well, although I suspect most people assume that the "terrible" part has to do with sex.

The information about her in the Bible has little to do with sex. Primarily the story is about cruelty and about the danger of worshiping the wrong god, a fatal flaw when wild dogs are on the prowl.

God became angry with Israel when Solomon was king. Remember Solomon, the wise and wonderful? In his old age he forgot how to think for himself and was influenced into worshiping false gods by his thousand foreign wives and concubines. This pattern continued through the reigns of Rehoboam, Jeroboam, Nadab, Baasha, Elah, Zimri, and Omri, right on down to Ahab. Over and over God insisted that God was the only God. Over and over kings married foreign wives, built shrines on the hills, worshiped their goddesses, and set bad examples for the rest of the country.

Then Ahab became king and "did more to provoke the LORD, the God of Israel, to anger than all the kings of Israel who were before Him" (1 Kings 16:33). Not only did he take the foreign woman

Jezebel as his wife, but Ahab built altars to Baal and Asherah, and he encouraged the 450 prophets of Baal and the 400 prophets of Asherah who came to dinner at the palace every night.

God was most disturbed by these goings on. God was utterly beside Godself when Ahab decided he wanted to buy the vineyards next to the royal palace. Naboth, the owner, refused to sell. Dutiful Jezebel didn't want her man to be unhappy and took matters into her own hands. She falsely accused Naboth of blasphemy and treason. As a result, he and his sons were stoned to death. Since no heirs were left to inherit, the land reverted to the king, Ahab.

Elijah, the local prophet, stopped by shortly afterward to let Ahab know that God had had enough. Dogs would lick up Ahab's blood and eat Jezebel and any other family members who died in the city. Birds would eat any kin who died in the open.

Jezebel died well, if horrifically. Aware that Jehu was being sent by Elijah to kill her, the queen dressed herself in fine robes and shadowed her eyes, as was her custom. Then she waited beside a window. Jehu did not kill her. Instead, he convinced her eunuchs to do the job by throwing her out the window. Dogs devoured her carcass, leaving only her feet, the palms of her hands, and her skull.

Quite a story, isn't it? Sounds like the precursor to *A Nightmare on Elm Street* or a living nightmare when you forget it's a Bible story and start thinking about current events, about MIAs and bomb blasts, and how awful it must be for all the folk who can't bury the bodies of their dead.

Nobody has spent much time lamenting Jezebel's death. In fact, popular wisdom's view of her seems to be rooted in sixteenth century slang, "when painting the face was accepted as prima-facie evidence that a woman had loose morals"[1] and "Jezebel" was the nickname awarded such a woman.

So what can we do with the real Jezebel, the sinning queen married to a man whose God preferred another wife for him? We could spend weeks lamenting the fact that Ahab and his fellow kings got off the hook for their sins, while Jezebel still is a figure of contempt, but it might be more profitable to use Jezebel's myth as a starting point for the consideration of our own attitudes toward sexuality.

Mores have changed in the past twenty years, so I'll restate what seems to me to have been the prevailing attitudes toward sex when baby boomers were coming of age. This is the way I remember it:

> Sex was wrong outside of marriage.
>
> Men who had sex outside of marriage couldn't help their natural urges.
>
> Women who had sex outside of marriage were bad.
>
> Women could be partially forgiven their badness in having sex as long as they hated themselves for it.
>
> A corollary for women of faith was that if you had sex outside of marriage, God would (maybe) forgive you if you hated yourself sufficiently. This is the heterosexual perspective; I imagine (although I don't remember any discussions at the time on the subject) an exponentially increased amount of self-hatred was considered the Christian requirement for lesbians.

I didn't realize what atrocious theology this was until I wrote it out. Jezebel thus opened for me some windows that had long been draped in crepe.

One evening I was talking with a friend who is a member of a twelve-step program (a spiritually based recovery program that originated with Alcoholics Anonymous and has expanded to include many other dysfunctional and obsessive behavior patterns; a hallmark of these programs is an acknowledgment of a "higher power," or God as each person understands the concept of God). My friend had seen her therapist that day and talked with her about the higher power.

Near the end of the conversation, the therapist had said, "It seems to me that your higher power is fear."

"She's right," said my friend. "I don't make choices based on what's best for me or on the way I want to live my life. I make choices based on what's the least scary option."

I think of that conversation regularly, especially now that I know I once (not so long ago) believed in a god who loved best those who hated themselves most. I work at understanding the difference between God who is a source of comfort and order vs. a god helpless in a chaotic universe. Intellectually, I have all this straight, but I have to work continually to keep the light shining in my dark corners.

I am perfectly capable of believing in a God of love and yet making fear my higher power. I did so for years. How did it feel? Oh, not so bad. Yes, I was frequently anxious and irritated and troubled, and I thought life drudgery and chaos, but there are no magic wands in adult existence. Some people I knew had a different version of reality: they thought that with a superficial change (a different house, an expensive pair of boots, a Jaguar, twenty pounds lost, bigger breasts) they wouldn't have these irritations, anxieties, and troubles. A magic wand would make their lives better without them having to make any changes in themselves. They and I, in dissimilar ways, compared our lives to magical existences and felt bereft.

See? Wild dogs are always on the prowl.

* * *

Look for God in Your Life

This idea comes from *Letting Go with Love* by Julia H.[2] Get a small notebook and each day list three things you're grateful for. Then list three things you did well.

The exercise sounds simple, but I learned a lot about myself from it. First, I saw that I was often too involved with how much the dog was shedding and who forgot to write "milk" on the grocery list to notice the wonders happening around me. Secondly, about the twentieth time I listed "brushing my teeth" under "Things I Did Well," it got through to me that I am very, very critical of myself. Third, knowing I had the list to complete each night, I spent time each day focused on the gifts of love and beauty that surround me.

After a few weeks, consider what you've accomplished by this task. Has your attitude toward the world changed? Is your attitude toward yourself changing? What is there of God in celebrating the world and yourself?

Herodias

And the moral of the story is: women are hateful.

Popular Wisdom

Herod and Herodias were a wicked couple. He left his wife to marry her, and she left her husband, Herod's brother, to marry him. Herodias had a daughter, sometimes called Salome, who could really shake that thing, with veils. One day, overcome by Salome's performance, Herod made a magnanimous offer.

"Tell me your dearest wish," he said, "and I will grant it."

Any of us who faced a fairy godmother offering three wishes might want some help in our decision. Salome, being young and without benefit of a phone to call friends for advice, asked her mom.

Mom didn't hesitate.

"Ask for John the Baptist's head."

This John was a weirdo. He wandered around in a camel's skin, eating locusts and forecasting the end of the world. Herodias hated him because John criticized her marital arrangements, accusing her and Herod of living in sin because of their messy divorces.

She saw her chance to shut John up. She took it.

John's head was carried in on a platter.

And the moral of the story is: women are hateful.

A Formal Feeling

In another life I watched
her dance, heard Herod
swear his oath.
She came to me, my daughter
dancing still, her prize
a token freely offered.

I was giddy with wine
and her success and the heat
and the smoke
from the tapers and love.
It wasn't the fun
I thought it would be,
even though I despised the wild
and woolly man who dared
chastize a king.
People listened,
as they always will
to tales of the lives
of the rich and famous.

Gaul's not bad, as places go.
I'm no longer queen.
Herod has headaches.
I don't feel at home.
I have no friends.
Yet the sun still comes up,
I still lay my head on a pillow
at night,
and life still waits
to see if I'll live it or not.

* * * * *

Funny about Herodias. She's so wicked that you'd expect popular wisdom to have a field day with her. In truth, while some traditions teach about her, many are silent to the point that people don't know how to pronounce her name. Maybe that's because she's too evil to be mentioned. Maybe she's hidden to protect our delicate sensibilities. Or maybe a woman capable of killing an enemy in a hate-filled rage is just too threatening to storytellers.

That's a shame, because hateful Herodias, due to the very explosiveness of her anger, is a good subject for contemplation.

I hang around with some Christian women who aren't too crazy about men. In fact, the word "hate" comes up in conversation. I don't worry about their ideas influencing me adversely because I agree with them.

I've hesitated, wiffled and waffled over whether identifying myself as a generic manhater is appropriate in a book meant to encourage love of oneself and others. But Christian duty sometimes requires that we venture into No Man's Land and describe the scenery. I'm buttressed by the knowledge that this isn't a peculiar wild hair of mine but an issue I hear other go-to-church-each-Sunday women struggling with.

I'm also buttressed by Beverly Wildung Harrison's remarks on Christian moral theology. She states that anger needs to be expressed because "all serious human moral activity . . . takes its bearings from the rising power of human anger. Such anger is a signal that change is called for, that transformation in relation is required."[1]

If we say "I hate men" loudly enough, insisting that this is a Christian problem, not just female trouble, maybe transformation can begin. Maybe men, and in particular Christian men, will recognize that their attitudes and actions are contributing to the supply of misery in the world and will take some responsibility for change.

What's the source of my hatred and anger? Self-preservation. Physical, financial, and emotional self-preservation makes hating men eminently reasonable.

Why? First, because the overwhelming majority of hired killers, soldiers of fortune, murderers, rapists, spouse beaters — people, that is, who make their living or pass their time by inflicting bodily harm — are men. It behooves me to recognize that men are dangerous. They are larger. They are stronger. Their upper body strength is greater. They're awash in testosterone. I don't love grizzly bears, cocaine, or men. This caution isn't enough to insure my physical safety, but it helps.

Why? Because economic power is in the hands of men. In 1975 the plant engineer I worked for said to me, "I'll raise your salary to match that of the man who's doing the same job when you go to Sweden and have a sex-change operation." Rumor has it such blatant discrimination has gone underground. Maybe, but a letter to the editor of *Ms.* magazine in 1989[2] tells us of an upper-level manager listening to her boss in a meeting say (heartily, I assume, with smiles all around), "Well, she's a woman; she can't be a genius."

Why? Because statistics tell us that women do two-thirds of the world's labor, receive one-tenth of its income, and control one per cent of its wealth, and that, upon divorce, men's standards of living rise and women's (along with their children's) plummet.

Why? Because those in power — most often white males — use their power to oppress. In Psych 101 I learned of an experiment in which a prison environment was simulated, with one group of students as guards and the other as prisoners. The changes in behavior — the cruelty that developed on the part of the "guards" in a very short time — required the experiment to be halted before somebody got hurt. Patriarchy and the white male power system have been acting out this experiment for thousands of years, and nobody as yet has managed to call it off, even though people are continually hurt.

Why? Because I'm plain old sick and tired of news reports that women can't preach because of Eve or can't participate in Lenten foot-washing ceremonies because of their gender. And I'm insulted when the powerholders making these pronouncements wonder why women don't shut up and meekly obey.

I have a fine point of connection with Herodias. In truth, I have moments when I wonder why all men's heads can't be cut off and served up on platters.

I'm not advocating lawlessness or murder. Yet I do understand the rage and bitterness, the combination of impulsivity and overpowering anger that led Herodias to dispatch John the Baptist. From that perspective the labels "good" and "bad" for her lose their meaning. Herodias instead is a symbol of mixed feelings, of lightning and dark, anger and love, and the question becomes how we can channel the range of feeling to bring about necessary change.

One final word on my attitude toward men. It opens me to grace in unexpected ways. When Barbara Harris was elected suffragan bishop of the Episcopal Diocese of Massachusetts, a man wrote to *The Witness*[3] and talked about his mother. He said that when he was elected bishop, she knit him a pair of purple bedroom slippers (I picture them with huge purple balls on the toes). His turned out nicely, so she continued to knit purple slippers for each bishop elected. Then her eyesight began to fail. It was time for her to stop knitting.

The bishop asked his mother a favor before she put away her needles. Would she make one last pair, a pair that he could save to give to the first woman elected bishop?

His mother said yes. Now she's 81 years old, and Barbara Harris has a pair of purple bedroom slippers.

I savor this story. It tells me that women are not alone in their vision of God's inclusive love, that some men have also noticed that this love is a vast and powerful thing. It tells me that moments of grace occur every day in kitchens and dining rooms, in front of television sets and beside baskets of worsted. It convinces me that we can lead each other beside still waters, and our souls can be restored.

* * *

Look for the Extraordinary

Two of Herodias's choices after the death of John the Baptist were to waste her life in self-hatred or to accept her failure and live. The following exercise is a tool I began using at a time when I felt myself a failure.

The exercise? To note the miraculous in each day.

I define miracles broadly. For me they range from a falling star to a pink cab on a garbage truck to a driver waving me on in traffic. The unusual, the bizarre, the new, the extraordinary — all these things count.

This exercise is one of waiting and trusting: waiting to see what glory the day has to offer and trusting that God intends for you to notice. Jot down these observations each day if that will help you notice and remember them.

Ask yourself these questions: Do I believe there's a spot of glory in each day? Is God capable of presenting these things for me to appreciate? How will my perspective change if I discipline myself to appreciate the world? What does this tell me about my attitude toward myself and God?

6

Martha

And the moral of the story is: whatever women do is wrong.

Popular Wisdom

Mary and Jesus were having an absolutely fascinating discussion about God.

Martha was stomping around banging clay pots together and muttering under her breath. Suddenly, her bad temper got the best of her.

"Mary!" she yelled, "Get in here and help me!"

"Why, Martha," said Jesus, "I'm surprised at you! What Mary's doing is important; what you're doing isn't."

And the moral of the story is: whatever women do is wrong.

I Am Woman.
Hear Me.

I can simultaneously
smile at my sister
check a child's head
for fever
ascertain that the bread
is not burning
urge the cat from the door
with the toe of my sandal
note that the hem
of my robe is torn
and talk to you
of things visible,
invisible, and
as yet undreamed.

I may seem scattered
but if you should call
when my sister is not here
when the child is not here
when the bread is not baking
and the cat not at the door
then I will sit down
and talk to you
of things visible,
invisible, and
as yet undreamed.

* * * * *

Discovering the truth behind the veil of popular wisdom is like picking through boxes at a garage sale: you have to toss aside layers of tattered and ragged junk in order to find the yard of pure silk. That's what I have to do with Martha.

The popular wisdom story that begins this chapter represents my earliest understanding of this scene. Martha was a monster-mother, an ogre insisting that Mary interrupt a visit with a dear friend in order to do some tiresome chore.

Martha seemed a jealous fault-finder. Mary's desire to learn was noble; Martha's efforts to force her to perform prosaic tasks were petty. I'd already figured out that housework was tedious and repetitive, its necessity recognized but its value denied.

Some time later, my sympathies lodged with Martha. Feeding people was one of her jobs, and she reasonably wanted Jesus, an honored guest, to be fed quickly and well. Mary was a flibbertigibbet — yes, listening to Jesus was important, but she had no business ignoring her duty.

Later I realized that this story can be mighty useful in scorning women. Our newspapers are filled with voices insisting that employed women are a new scourge, neglecting their children and purposefully destroying the fabric of society. Yet women who stay home (including but not limited to welfare mothers) are, like the Martha of popular wisdom, thought too dull to recognize there's more to life than housework.

Now that I'm older, calmer, and more appreciative of sisters, I see this story differently. I now know that when Jesus said, "Martha, Martha, you are anxious and troubled about many things; one thing is needful. Mary has chosen the good portion which shall not be taken away from her" (Luke 10:41b-42), he was asserting women's worth. In a society that considered women property and on a par with camels when it came to brains, Jesus affirmed their godliness and their right to study and learn. Jesus was making a radical statement for his time, not setting women up for conflicts between home and career.

I also know now about another scene in Martha's life, described in John 11:25-27:

> Jesus said to her [Martha], "I am the resurrection and the life; he who believes in me, though he die, yet shall he live, and whoever lives and believes in me shall never die. Do you believe this?" She said to him, "Yes, Lord; I believe that you are the Christ, the Son of God, he who is coming into the world."

In *The Women Around Jesus*, Elisabeth Moltmann-Wendell explains the significance of this scene. She says, "This is a confession of Christ which takes similar form only once more in the other Gospels, where it is uttered by Peter. . . . The church was built up on Peter's confession, and to this day the Popes understand themselves as Peter's successors."[1]

Martha is thus a crucial figure in Jesus' ministry. Peter's confession is seen as the basis for apostolic succession. As respect for Bible women increases, and we begin to call their experience sacred, Martha's confession may well become a focus for laypeople, and we will claim ourselves as her successors.

But let's get back to the better known scene in Martha's life, the one that seems to set in conflict her role as homebody and Mary's as student, which I'm going to address as the conflict between caregiving and career. Most women today juggle those two roles. Just like Martha, we're trying to feed people's bodies and our own souls at the same time and often end up frustrated in the attempt.

I heard this stated most plainly in a recent conversation with a woman who, with her husband, had adopted two Korean children ages seven and five. The new mom was still in the process of adjustment.

"What's the hardest part?" I asked.

She said there were two hard parts. One was the awesome responsibility. She described lying in bed each night asking, "Why did I do this? Should I have said that? Am I doing everything I can?" The second hard part was her sense that she'd lost touch with herself because she no longer had any private time. It was as though she'd had to choose between being a human being and being a mother/caretaker.

She articulated what many of us face when nurturing responsibilities (whether for an infant, an older child, a spouse or a parent) suddenly command precedence in our lives. Must we choose between being Martha and being Mary? How do we make that choice?

Somehow we do, and very often guilt is the result. I have on my desk a letter from a friend with a husband, a toddler, and a full-time job. She says, "I feel guilty when I'm at work away from the baby. When I'm with the baby, I feel guilty because I can't give as much energy to my work as I think it requires." The woman who wrote this is mentally healthy, spiritually strong, and good-spirited, yet guilt pesters her all the livelong day.

Most of the women I know struggle with this effluvium. We act as though it's something real. I don't believe it is. I think guilt is a subsidiary response to our own harshness with ourselves. There may be a thousand interesting volumes on the library shelf, but we force ourselves to read the most suffocating autobiography — without even, as Alice in Wonderland noticed, the benefit of illustrations.

Here are some illustrations of how I think we should treat guilt:

Shove it into a bottle and send it out to sea (wave as it disappears in the waves).

Stuff it in the fireplace and strike a match.

Put it in the toe of an old tennis shoe, put the shoe in a trash bag, tie up the bag, and take it to the garbage can.

Put it in a box and drop it off at the post office.

Picture it coating your hands like crankshaft grease; wash your hands with Boraxo; then clean the sink.

See it embodied in the dress in your closet that you hate the most. Give it to the Salvation Army.

Picture it as a termite; then call pest control.

Picture it as a mean dog and watch a car run over it.

Now I've gone too far — or maybe I haven't yet gone far enough. At first I thought this an audacious exercise, and that the Femininity Police would break down my door for violating a code of honor. How dare I be whimsical about guilt? Now I think whimsy may be the most appropriate response.

How can guilt hold court when I'm amused by it? My joviality says to guilt, "You're not in charge here." It affirms that I love a God who loves me for being a woman, who celebrates my life, who wants me to celebrate my life because God is in it and of it. It insists that the time I spend in negativity about myself separates me from God in everything — and it requires me to refuse to do that chore.

Does this approach work? Sometimes better than others (I've been well conditioned), but, yes, it works.

I don't see the story of Martha and Mary as a study in conflict any longer. Instead I see Martha as the embodiment of the fullness of women's lives. The real Martha was worker and caregiver, self-loving and other-loving, bread-baker and confessor. The real Martha lets us define ourselves not as dwellers in impossibility but as creators of possibility for ourselves and others, as we stand in the sand, waving good-bye to a bottle of guilt sailing out to sea.

* * *

Make Time for Yourself: Begin a Journal

Keeping a journal is like reading the Bible: many of us intend to do it, but we can't quite get started. Do we need another chore added into our schedules? Is it worth it?

I believe it is. The Pilgrims settling in America had a purpose in keeping journals: they believed God was immanent, and they wanted a record of how God acted in their lives. I do it for that reason, too, and for sustenance on off-days, and because as a writer I need the practice, and because it helps me notice whether the view of myself I carry around in my back pocket agrees with what I believe is God's view of me.

Consider your own reasons. If you decide to begin, these steps may help:

1. *Decide on the mechanics.*

Do you prefer to write on legal pads or looseleaf notepaper? In bound blank books or in those with sayings? Lined or unlined? Choose a format that feels comfortable and pleasurable to you.

2. *Pick a time of day.*

Like Bible reading, journal keeping needs to be scheduled. If you're overbooked, look for stray moments: the time spent waiting in a doctor's office or in the school parking lot waiting for your children.

3. *Choose a method.*

I alternate, but the one I've found most effective is suggested by Natalie Goldberg in her book *Writing Down the Bones*.[2] She says to set a time period — fifteen minutes, half an hour, whatever — and for that period keep the pen moving across the paper. Don't stop and think. Don't worry about what you're saying. Just write.

You may choose to be more intentional. Some people record interesting stories they want to remember. Others focus on a Bible passage, or the day-to-day changes in their gardens, or on their reading. The journal then becomes a medium for deliberate reflection.

Mary
Magdalene

And the moral of the story is: women aren't good enough.

Popular Wisdom

Mary Magdalene was a prostitute. Jesus was the only one not poisoned by her mere presence.

Jesus healed her, and she left behind her disgusting ways. She turned out all right because of him.

She talked to a few people about Jesus after she saw the Resurrected One, but she never preached. Only Jewish men could preach. Not women. And certainly not prostitutes.

And the moral of the story is: women aren't good enough.

Say It, Sister!

I have this to say to one and all:
we are no longer strangers each to the other
we shall no longer call names
we shall not dance to a drum not our own
we shall not sing to a hymn not our own
we shall not point fingers
we shall not revile ourselves or others
we shall not be strangers

I have this to say:
our name is one name
our drum is one drum
our hymn is one hymn
our hands are clasped
our love is God's
we are the same

* * * * *

In a word-association test, if the test-giver said "Mary Magdalene," the most common response would likely be "prostitute." How steadfastly we cling to our ignorance. Bible commentators for decades have pointed out that Scripture says no such thing.

What does the Bible say about this woman? The earliest chronological reference is in Luke 8:1-2. This passage tells of Jesus preaching in the towns and villages. With him were the twelve disciples and several women, one of whom was "Mary, called Magdalene, from whom seven demons had come out."

The remainder of the biblical references to Mary concern her role at the resurrection, including the fact that she was the first person to whom Jesus appeared after the crucifixion. John 20:17b-18 says Jesus told Mary Magdalene to "'go to my brethren and say to them, I am ascending to my Father and your Father, to my God and your God.' Mary Magdalene went and said to the disciples, 'I have seen the Lord'; and she told them that he had said these things to her."

This scene is powerful. Jesus is making the first call for someone to preach the good news of the resurrection. It is the beginning — and the beginning rests with a woman.

How did we get from here to the myth of Mary Magdalene as a prostitute?

I can understand it best in terms of a short story I wrote several years ago.

*

When the angel Gabriel came to Mary, she quailed at sight of him.

"Be not afraid," spoke the angel. "I am come from the Lord to deliver great tidings. Unto you will be born a child to bring light into the darkness. Generations will rise up and call your babe blessed; its name will live forevermore."

Mary was greatly troubled but placed her faith in the Lord. She and the angel spoke at length and then retired, the one to return to God, the other to find Joseph, her affianced.

Joseph heard the story told by Mary and was filled with wonder. He, a poor man, to share in the miracle of the birth of a savior. . . . With firm steps, he led Mary to the house of her parents.

"The Lord has spoken. Mary carries a child who will bring peace on earth."

The wedding feast was held with much rejoicing.

At length the time came for Mary to be delivered. She and Joseph journeyed to Bethlehem and found shelter there. In the night sky appeared a wondrous star, leading shepherds and wise men to the stable where the baby lay.

The first shepherd looked into the face of Joseph and was sorely afraid.

"What child is this whose birth causes the angels to proclaim from on high?"

Joseph spat upon the ground; a great trembling wracked his shoulders.

"Is this not Mary, your wife, gone to childbed? Does not the light of the world wait here, in the manger, for us?"

Joseph spat once more and dragged a hand through the beard upon his face. "No child of mine lies here," spoke he, "nor wife of mine." He strode forth and disappeared into the night.

The shepherds and wise men came together, asking, "What manner of man is this, who can leave his wife, who can turn his back on the Lord and on our salvation?"

Greatly troubled, they approached Mary. Her face was still damp from childbirth; her eyes shone with the radiance of God's love.

The babe, wrapped in swaddling clothes, lay close at hand in a manger. Wise men and shepherds knelt in adoration. They placed gifts before the holy child. At last one wise man rose and offered his hand in thanksgiving to Mary.

"Verily, I say unto you, this is the Son of God. Praise to him, and to you who have entered into the miracle."

Mary brushed a tendril from her forehead with a weary hand and smiled. "All praise to God . . . but my child is not the Son of God."

Consternation flew across their faces like clouds before the moon.

"But the angel on high spoke to the shepherds; the star led us here to you. Doubt you, woman, the messages of your God?"

"I doubt not," said Mary. "God is here with us incarnate, but my child is not the Son of God. She is the Daughter of God, sent to cleanse us of our sins and lead us to the life everlasting."

In silence the men withdrew to consider these words. Then they gathered their entourages and rode into the night, their mouths sealed against this blasphemy. The final shepherd to leave, with many a cautious glance over his shoulder, hurled a torch into the stable. The straw, long dry, kindled quickly.

The blazing star hung low over the stable. Flames rose to

embrace it. The beacon shone long into the night.

Then the world sank into darkness.

After many generations, God, in great wisdom, sent another child to the weary earth. This one's name would be Jesus. He, at least, would be permitted to speak.

*

I wrote this story not long after my introduction to Christian feminism. I was teaching a Sunday school class on the topic and reading voluminously in preparation. I kept expecting to find this story in print, and, when it didn't turn up, wrote it myself. The thesis seemed so simple but so necessary to state: Jesus wasn't born male because God prefers baby boys. Jesus was born male because God had a message for the world and needed a messenger who could be heard.

How effective would a female Messiah have been? Could she have been educated in the Law? Would she have had access to the temple? Could she have had the freedom to wander from town to town? Who would have listened to a mere woman — even if that mere woman were the Messiah? The baby had to be a boy, not to prove the superiority of males, but to function in the society into which he was born.

This brings us back around to Mary Magdalene. Women's status did not take a sudden leap to equality because of Christ's ministry. This new sect, eager to follow Jesus' direction to witness to the ends of the earth, had first to survive in the society within which it was born. Although Jesus had made it abundantly clear that he was calling women to be prominent leaders, the new church caved in to the pressures of patriarchal society, conforming to and embracing its vision of the second-class status of women.

A more pointed explanation of Mary Magdalene's demotion comes from Rosemary Radford Ruether in *WomanGuides*. She says, "The Church paints a picture of Mary Magdalene as weeping sinner, thereby displacing her from her original high status as the leader of the faithful remnant of Jesus' apostles."[1] The gnostic Gospel of Mary, set aside when decisions were made as to which books to include in the New Testament, confirms Mary Magdalene as preacher and teacher.

So why the myth of Mary Magdalene, prostitute? Perhaps because men and women have always been adversaries in Western culture, and the easiest tactic for shutting up an opponent is to call her names. Cast enough stones upon her lifestyle, and her message will be buried along with her.

Yet Mary Magdalene hasn't been buried. She remains the woman healed by Jesus who chose to follow and to claim her faith. She remains a woman who understood her power.

When I was in Nairobi, I attended a session on women and faith and heard the word "power" tossed around like so much confetti — not frivolously but plentifully. The point the speakers were making eventually sunk in: someone, whether it be a minister, a committee, or popular wisdom, is deciding how our power will be used (where our donations will go, how the Bible will be interpreted, who will be served). Power is not intrinsically evil, said the speakers. God gives personal power to each of us, and each of us chooses whether we'll exercise that power or let it be usurped.

A few years ago magazines were full of articles about women being afraid of their own power. Supposedly we sabotaged ourselves because we were fearful of success. Then a new spate of articles came along, revealing that it isn't fear that slows us down but the crippling headaches we get from banging our heads against glass ceilings, the exhaustion we feel because although wives have joined the public workforce husbands haven't joined the private workforce at home, and the stress of trying to raise children to adulthood with too little time to think and less time to enjoy.

None of these circumstances are likely to change in the next five minutes. Society will continue to define women's roles and to limit our power. God will continue to give us opportunities to use the power we do have to its limits and beyond. The world will always be with us, and we will always have moments of strength and weakness, or shadow and light. Mary Magdalene teaches me that we must name and claim our power. We must grasp it, nuzzle it, nurture it, speak it, celebrate it, run with it, fly with it . . . use it in the best way we know how.

We can trust in God for the rest.

* * *

Pursue Your Own Bliss

In a television interview with Bill Moyers, Joseph Campbell said that when college students came to him asking what they should do with their lives (what major? what graduate school? what job?), he advised them to pursue their own bliss.

If we believe a good God created each of us for a purpose; if we believe we are given peculiar and extraordinary gifts; if we believe that we are necessary elements in the order of creation; if we believe that God works in mysterious ways and performs wonders; then we can believe that our interests, excitements, and heart-desires will reveal more of God's intention for us than any standard-profile test or analytical conclusion as to what career is best.

Consider these questions:

1. *What will happen if people choose to pursue their own bliss?*

Anarchy? Order? Happiness? What does your conclusion tell you about your view of God and the world?

2. *Are you now pursuing your own bliss?*

If not, why not? Are you too busy? Are you worried that you can't succeed? Are you afraid to take the risk? Are you concerned about what people might think?

3. *What aspect of your bliss are you pursuing today?*

Is it through supporting your family? Is it through doing your job well?

4. *Does celebrating our own lives help us celebrate God?*

Afterword

Some people speak of the communion of saints.

One day my daughter Tara, home on a visit from college, was sitting on the couch kissing Clyde, our cat.

"When are you going to outgrow that dirty habit?" asked Fred.

"There are only three cats I ever kiss," she said.

I knew which three she meant: Clyde in her lap; Bonnie, a cat we'd had for seven years, recently murdered by a neighborhood dog; and Ranger, Tara's own cat.

"Who are the three you kiss?" I asked anyhow.

"Clyde, Ranger, and Buck," she said — Buck being her sister Debbie's cat that had recently boarded with Tara for six months.

"Not Bonnie?" I asked.

"Not like this, Mama," she said. "Bonnie's getting angel kisses."

When I contracted to write this book, I was anxious for days. Could I really do this? Was it worth doing? Should I be the one to do it?

Then one night I had a dream. A woman who was very kind to me when I was a teenager was talking to me. She told me not to worry, that things were working out as they should, that all would be well. I remembered the dream the next morning, and I began again to trust.

Some people refer to the communion of saints. I like to think I'm getting angel kisses.

Notes

Introduction

1. Zora Neale Hurston, *Their Eyes Were Watching God* (Urbana: University of Illinois Press, 1978), 76.

2. Zsuzsanna E. Budapest, "Self-Blessing Ritual," in *Womanspirit Rising*, edited by Carol P. Christ and Judith Plaskow (San Francisco: Harper & Row, Publishers, Inc., 1979), 271.

3. Nelle Morton, "The Dilemma of Celebration," in *Womanspirit Rising*, edited by Christ and Plaskow, 159.

4. Katherine Anthony, *Susan B. Anthony: Her Personal History and Her Era* (Garden City, New York: Doubleday & Company, 1954), 438-39.

Eve

1. Marie Chapian, *Love and Be Loved* (Old Tappen, New Jersey: Fleming H. Revell Company, 1983), 43–45.

Lot's Wife

1. Edith Deen, *All of the Women of the Bible* (New York: Harper & Row, 1955), 17–19.

2. Deen, *Ibid.*, 18.

Delilah

1. Helen Lee Turner, Amy E. Jones, and Doris A. Blazer, "The Hanna-Barbera Cartoons: Compounding Bible Ignorance?" *The Christian Century*, 106 (1 March 1989): 232.

Jezebel

1. Deen, *All of the Women of the Bible*, 131.
2. Julia H., *Letting Go with Love* (Los Angeles: Jeremy P. Tarcher, Inc., 1987), 43.

Herodias

1. Beverly Wildung Harrison, "The Power of Anger in the Work of Love: Christian Ethics for Women and Other Strangers," in *Weaving the Visions: New Patterns in Feminist Spirituality*, edited by Judith Plaskow and Carol P. Christ (San Francisco: Harper & Row, Publishers, 1989), 220.
2. "Renaissance Artist," *Ms.*, 17 (January/February 1989): 14.
3. John S. Spong, Bishop of Newark, Letter to the Editor, *The Witness*, 71 (November 1988): 7

Martha

1. Elisabeth Moltmann-Wendell, *The Women Around Jesus* (New York: Crossroad, 1982), 25.
2. Natalie Goldberg, *Writing Down the Bones* (Boston: Shambhala, 1986), 8.

Mary Magdalene

1. Rosemary Radford Ruether, *WomanGuides* (Boston: Beacon Press, 1985), 178.

Mary Cartledge-Hayes

Mary Cartledge-Hayes is a South Carolinian who grew up on an island in Lake Erie.

Her enthusiasm for the melding of the secular and sacred in individual lives has led her to leadership positions in both feminist and church women's organizations. She attended the 1985 women's conferences in Nairobi, Kenya.

A free-lance writer, she has written Sunday school curriculum for elementary children for the United Methodist Publishing House. In addition, Cartledge-Hayes has had published nearly one hundred poems, short stories, and essays in such magazines and journals as *Daughters of Sarah, The Christian Century, The Upper Room, Ms.,* and *Southern Feminist.*

Adriana Diaz

Adriana Diaz is a graphic artist, painter, ceramist, and writer. With a master's degree in spirituality and culture, she is currently on the faculty of the Institute of Culture and Creation Spirituality at Holy Names College in Oakland, where she teaches painting and clay as meditation.

Her first book, a guide to painting and drawing as transformational arts, will be published by Harper and Row in the spring of 1991.

LuraMedia Publications

BANKSON, MARJORY ZOET
  Braided Streams: *Esther and a Woman's Way of Growing*
  Seasons of Friendship: *Naomi and Ruth as a Pattern*

BOHLER, CAROLYN STAHL
  Prayer on Wings: *A Search for Authentic Prayer*

BOZARTH, ALLA RENEE
  Womanpriest: *A Personal Odyssey (Rev. Ed.)*

GEIGER, LURA JANE
  Astonish Me, Yahweh Leader's Guide

  and **PATRICIA BACKMAN**
  Braided Streams Leader's Guide

  and **SUSAN TOBIAS**
  Seasons of Friendship Leader's Guide

  and **SANDY LANDSTEDT, MARY GECKELER, PEGGIE OURY**
  Astonish Me, Yahweh!: *A Bible Workbook-Journal*

JEVNE, RONNA FAY
  It All Begins With Hope: *Patients, Caretakers, and the Bereaved Speak Out*

  and **ALEXANDER LEVITAN**
  No Time for Nonsense: *Getting Well Against the Odds*

KEIFFER, ANN
  Gift of the Dark Angel: *A Woman's Journey through Depression toward Wholeness*

LODER, TED
  Eavesdropping on the Echoes: *Voices from the Old Testament*
  Guerrillas of Grace: *Prayers for the Battle*
  No One But Us: *Personal Reflections on Public Sanctuary*
  Tracks in the Straw: *Tales Spun from the Manger*
  Wrestling the Light: *Ache and Awe in the Human-Divine Struggle*

LUCIANI, JOSEPH
  Healing Your Habits: *Introducing Directed Imagination*

MCMAKIN, JACQUELINE
  with **SONYA DYER**
  Working from the Heart: *For Those Who Search for Meaning and Satisfaction in Their Work*

MEYER, RICHARD C.
  One Anothering: *Biblical Building Blocks for Small Groups*

MILLETT, CRAIG
  In God's Image: *Archetypes of Women in Scripture*

O'CONNOR, ELIZABETH
  Search for Silence *(Revised Edition)*

RAFFA, JEAN BENEDICT
  The Bridge to Wholeness: *A Feminine Alternative to the Hero Myth*

SAURO, JOAN
  Whole Earth Meditation: *Ecology for the Spirit*

SCHAPER, DONNA
  A Book of Common Power: *Narratives Against the Current*
  Stripping Down: *The Art of Spiritual Restoration*

WEEMS, RENITA J.
  Just a Sister Away: *A Womanist Vision of Women's Relationships in the Bible*

The Women's Series

BORTON, JOAN
  Drawing from the Women's Well: *Reflections from the Life Passage of Menopause*

CARTLEDGE-HAYES, MARY
  To Love Delilah: *Claiming the Women of the Bible*

DAHL, JUDY
  River of Promise: *Two Women's Story of Love and Adoption*

DUERK, JUDITH
  Circle of Stones: *Woman's Journey to Herself*

RUPP, JOYCE
  The Star in My Heart: *Experiencing Sophia, Inner Wisdom*

SCHAPER, DONNA
  Superwoman Turns 40: *The Story of One Woman's Intentions to Grow Up*

LuraMedia, Inc. , 7060 Miramar Rd., Suite 104, San Diego, CA 92121
Books for Healing and Hope, Balance and Justice.